My family celebrates
Christmas

Cath Senker

Photography by Chris Fairclough

W

FRANKLIN WATTS
LONDON · SYDNEY

First published in 2009 by
Franklin Watts
338 Euston Road
London NW1 3BH

Franklin Watts Australia
Level 17/207 Kent Street
Sydney NSW 2000

Copyright © 2009 Franklin Watts

ISBN: 978 0 7496 9061 8

Dewey classification number: 394.26'63

Planning and production by Discovery Books Limited
Editor: Laura Durman
Designer: Ian Winton
Photography by Chris Fairclough

The author and photographer would like to acknowledge the following for their help in preparing this book: Stephen Anderson,
Lucy Grout, Chad and Finn Anderson-Grout; Lucas and Philip Meldrum, and Pilar Teran. We would like to thank the congregation
at St Nicholas Church, Brighton, and in particular: Father Robert Chavner, Lynn Rashid, Peggy Guggenheim, Joanne Morrell and
the children of the Junior Church (Sunday school); Anne Cross. Special thanks to Joanne Morrell for the loan of the Nativity scene.
The recipe on pages 20–21 is from Waitrose.com.

Please note, the way that people celebrate festivals varies and this book represents the experience of one family. It should not be
assumed that everyone celebrates in the same way.

Printed in China

Franklin Watts is a division of Hachette Children's Books, an Hachette UK company.
www.hachette.co.uk

Words that appear in **bold** in the text are explained in the glossary.

Contents

Globe panels

People celebrate Christmas in lots of different ways around the world. Look out for the globe panels for some examples.

About my family and me

My name is Finn and I'm eight. My brother Chad is 10. We live with our mum and dad and two cats, Titian and Raphy. I love swimming – my brother and I go to swimming club twice a week. I also like playing on my bike and scooter.

Here's my family outside our house. I'm at the front on the right.

My family are Christian and I go to a Christian school. Every Sunday we go to **church** and **Sunday school**.

This book will show you how my family celebrates the Christian festival of Christmas.

I love going out on my scooter with Chad.

The festival of Christmas

Christians worship Jesus as the Son of God. At Christmas we celebrate his birth. Long ago, an **angel** told a woman called Mary that she was going to have a special baby.

At Sunday school we make a collage of the **Nativity scene**.

Germany

Making **Christingles** is a German tradition to teach children about Jesus. This is what the parts mean: Orange — the world. Candle — Jesus, the light of the world. Cocktail sticks — the four seasons. Red ribbon — Jesus' blood. Fruit and sweets — the fruit of the Earth. Today, children in Britain often make Christingles, too.

I put raisins on my Christingle.

Months later, Mary and her husband Joseph had to travel to Bethlehem to pay a **tax**. When they arrived, there were no rooms to stay in. They sheltered in a stable. That night, Jesus was born.

Advent

Advent is the period of four weeks before Christmas. Advent means 'coming' – the coming of Jesus. During Advent we prepare to celebrate the birth of Jesus.

In church there is an Advent **wreath** with five candles. We light a candle every Sunday leading up to Christmas. On Christmas Day we light the last one.

The **vicar** watches as I light the Advent candles in church.

We count the days until Christmas using **Advent calendars** and candles. Our cats each have an Advent calendar too!

Advent is a time of hope. We hope for a better world.

Mum helped us to make an Advent wreath. Chad hangs it on our front door.

Preparing for Christmas

Before Christmas we go shopping for presents for our friends and family. We buy a real Christmas tree. We put it up in the living room and decorate it.

I love decorating the Christmas tree.

We write Christmas cards to our friends and family.

My friend Lucas and I write our Christmas cards.

The day before Christmas is Christmas Eve. Chad and I go to bed early – we can't wait for Christmas morning!

Bolivia

On Christmas Eve in Bolivia, the church bells ring to call people to **Mass** at midnight. At the service, they celebrate the birth of Jesus. Then they return home for a big Christmas feast. It is summer, so people have drinks with ice to keep them cool.

Christmas Day!

On Christmas morning Chad and I get up early. We are allowed to open the small presents in our **Christmas stockings**. When Mum and Dad get up, we all have breakfast. Then we put on our smart clothes.

As soon as we wake up, we rush downstairs to see what is in our Christmas stockings.

We go for a short walk before going to church. Normally we go to Sunday school with all the other children. On Christmas Day there is a special family service for everyone.

We walk near our church. It is old and beautiful.

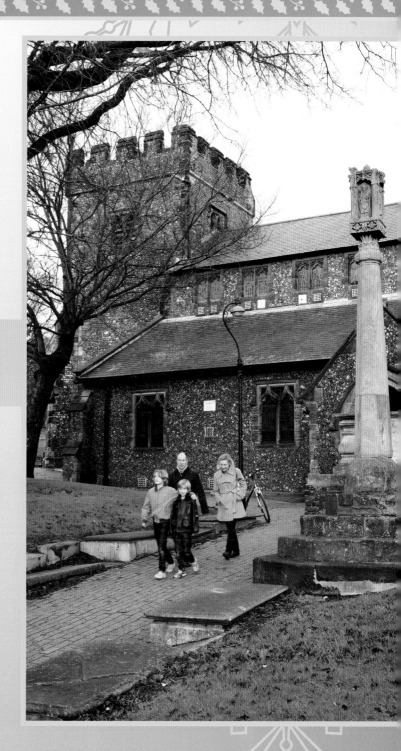

Spain

In Spain, children don't have presents on Christmas Day. The day for giving presents is **Epiphany** on 6 January. On this day, the **Three Kings** brought gifts for the baby Jesus.

Going to church

The church is full on Christmas Day. Our vicar, Father Robert, reads from the **Bible** about the birth of Jesus and gives his Christmas **sermon**. He talks about how we can all try to be kinder to each other and work for peace in the world.

Father Robert says we should thank God for giving us his only Son.

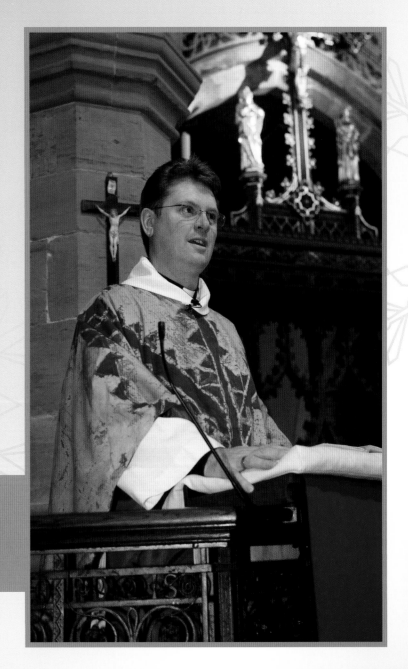

Father Robert leads the **Eucharist** service. People come up to take a little piece of bread and some wine, which helps them to remember Jesus. The service feels very special on Christmas Day.

After Eucharist, we say prayers and sing Christmas **carols**.

We sing my favourite carol, 'Away in a Manger'.

Christmas dinner

After church, my friend Lucas comes to our house with his parents. Dad has cooked a delicious Christmas dinner.

We raise our glasses and wish each other a Merry Christmas.

Christmas food in Europe

The traditional British Christmas dinner includes turkey, roast potatoes, Brussels sprouts, cranberry sauce and Christmas pudding.

In Russia, people eat twelve special dishes. The dishes stand for Jesus' twelve **Apostles**.

In Sicily, it is traditional to eat eels at Christmas time.

People in Poland eat mushroom soup on Christmas Eve.

Stollen is a popular Christmas bread in Austria, Germany and Switzerland.

Our family does not eat meat, so we have fish. We eat baked salmon, roast potatoes, red cabbage and sprouts. For tea we'll have Christmas cake.

This picture shows a traditional British Christmas dinner. Finn's family do not have turkey because they do not eat meat.

Christmas fun

After dinner, we are allowed to open our big presents and play with our new toys.

Mum and dad buy us a big present each.

Australia

As Christmas is in the summer in Australia, people often have Christmas parties on the beach. Many have a picnic or barbecue, with seafood or steaks and salad. They swim in the sea and play beach games.

Lucas gave me a game of Ludo for Christmas.
We decide to play it straight away!

Our family loves singing, so we sing some carols.
We think about baby Jesus coming into the world.

Later, before it gets dark, we go for a short walk. Then,
like most other families, we settle down in front of the TV.

A Christmas recipe: festive fairy cakes

Instead of mince pies, we eat special Christmas fairy cakes with a little **mincemeat** mixed in. Ask an adult to help you to make them.

You will need
- 125g unsalted butter, softened
- 75g caster sugar
- 2 large eggs, beaten
- 125g self-raising flour
- 1 × 410g jar mincemeat
- 1 tsp baking powder
- 225g icing sugar
- 100g tub glacé cherries

1. Preheat the oven to 190°C (gas mark 5). Put 16 paper cases in two bun tins.

2. Beat the butter and sugar until pale and creamy. Then whisk in the eggs a little at a time.

3. Fold in the flour, mincemeat and baking powder. Put a little of the mixture in each paper case.

4. Bake for 15–20 minutes until the cakes are golden and firm. Move them to a wire rack to cool.

5. Make the icing using the instructions on the packet. Spoon it over the cakes. Smooth the icing with a round-ended knife.

6. Put a cherry on each cake.

Glossary

Advent 'Coming'. The four weeks before Christmas, when Christians prepare for the festival.

Advent calendar A special calendar used to count the days of Advent.

angel Christians believe an angel is a messenger from God.

Apostles Twelve men that Jesus chose to tell other people about his teachings.

Bible The holy book of the Christian religion.

carols Religious songs that are sung at Christmas time.

Christingle An object made from an orange, a candle, four cocktail sticks with sweets or raisins on the end, and a red ribbon.

Christmas stocking A decoration that is shaped like a large sock. Christmas stockings are often filled with small presents.

church The Christian place of worship.

Epiphany A festival on 6 January. Christians remember when the Three Kings came to see the baby Jesus and offered him gifts.

Eucharist A church ceremony. People eat a little bread and drink some wine to remember Jesus. The bread stands for his body and the wine stands for his blood.

Mass The Roman Catholic name for the Eucharist ceremony.

mincemeat A mixture of dried fruit and spices used as a filling for pies, especially at Christmas.

Nativity scene A model of the baby Jesus and his family in the stable where he was born.

sermon A talk given by a church leader.

Sunday school A class at church on a Sunday where children learn about being Christian.

tax Money that people have to pay to the government so that it can run the country.

Three Kings The Three Kings, also called the Three Wise Men, followed a bright star to find the baby Jesus. They brought him gifts.

vicar The person who is in charge of a church and the area around it.

wreath An arrangement of leaves and flowers, often in the shape of a circle.

Finding out more

Books

Read and Learn: Christmas by Jennifer Gillis (Raintree Publishers, 2004)

Start-up Religion: Gifts at Christmas (Evans Brothers, 2004)

Why Is This Festival Special?: Christmas by Jillian Powell (Franklin Watts, 2009)

Special Days of the Year: Christmas by Katie Dicker (Wayland, 2009)

We Love Christmas by Saviour Pirotta (Wayland, 2009)

CD-Rom

Our Places of Worship, produced by Wayland.

This CD-Rom explores six major religions found in Britain. Each religion is introduced by a child who follows the faith.

Websites

http://infants.reonline.org.uk/

Look up Christmas in the festivals section to find out what Christmas means, how people celebrate, and how to make a Christingle.

http://www.request.org.uk/main/festivals/christmas/christmas01.htm

The RE:Quest website, with information pages, activities and puzzles.

http://www.woodlands-junior.kent.sch.uk/customs/Xmas/index.html

Links to information about the meaning of Christmas and about how people celebrate.

http://www.woodlands-junior.kent.sch.uk/teacher/christmas.html#world

Links to websites about how Christmas is celebrated in different countries.

Note to parents and teachers: Every effort has been made by the Publishers to ensure that these websites are suitable for children, that they are of the highest educational value, and that they contain no inappropriate or offensive material. However, because of the nature of the Internet, it is impossible to guarantee that the contents of these sites will not be altered. We strongly advise that Internet access is supervised by a responsible adult.

Index